BOYS, GIRLS &
P(

C000072068

By Ian Smith

Cartoons:
Phil Hailstone

Published by:

Teachers' Pocketbooks
Laurel House, Station Approach,
Alresford, Hampshire SO24 9JH, UK
Tel: +44 (0)1962 735573
Fax: +44 (0)1962 733637
E-mail: sales@teacherspocketbooks.co.uk
Website: www.teacherspocketbooks.co.uk

*Teachers' Pocketbooks is an imprint of
Management Pocketbooks Ltd.*

Series editor – Linda Edge.

© Ian Smith 2010.

This edition published 2010.
Revised reprint 2015.

ISBN 978 1 906610 24 1

E-book ISBN 978 1 908284 64 8

British Library Cataloguing-in-Publication
Data – A catalogue record for this book is
available from the British Library.

Design, typesetting and graphics by **efex Ltd**.
Printed in UK.

Contents

Foreword

How boys and girls should be educated is a topic that provokes vigorous, emotive debate. People hold very strong and very different views. Some believe that boys and girls should go to the same schools and learn in mixed gender classes and mixed gender groups. Others think the exact opposite: that both girls and boys will be more focused on learning when taught in separate schools, separate classes and separate groups.

This pocketbook doesn't advocate one view or the other. Based on current understandings about motivation, gender and learning, it looks at practical ways to help both boys and girls be motivated to learn.

Foreword

The book is based on two key premises:

1. **Gender is one of our most deep-seated traits.** There are very real differences between men and women, girls and boys. These differences need to be acknowledged, accepted and exploited for education purposes.

2. **But we are not from 'different planets'** as that popular book would have us believe. Boys are from earth and so are girls! There are more similarities between the genders than differences. The differences don't apply to everyone and, most importantly, we don't need to see them as limitations.

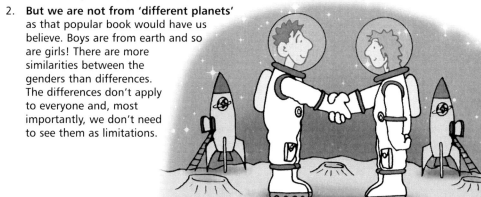

Foreword

There are innate differences between the average man and woman, the average girl and boy. The genders think, feel, behave, communicate and learn differently, and there is increasing evidence that these differences are particularly significant when the brain is developing in the early and teenage years.

In the past, our desire to affirm women and to ensure gender equality has led us to play down these differences. To do so does both genders a disservice: learning and teaching cannot be 'gender blind'.

Pupils come into class with assumptions about gender roles imposed on them by society as a whole. Learning more about gender differences and the impact they have in the classroom is essential for all teachers. With such knowledge, teachers are better able to motivate both boys and girls to learn. They are also better equipped to help them mature into confident adults who are comfortable with their own femininity or masculinity and able to relate effectively and appropriately to other men and women.

Foreword

Motivation, gender and learning are a complex mix and this Pocketbook does not advocate simple solutions to complicated issues. The dangers of stereotyping are obvious. Recognising that boys or girls are different can very easily turn into an excuse for saying that either gender is superior or defective in some way. Or that boys or girls can't help their behaviours.

Obviously, gender differences are not cut and dried. The message is not that teachers should expect 'girls to be girls' or 'boys to be boys'. Some boys are more masculine than others and some girls are more feminine than others. Throughout, when referring to boys or girls, I'm talking about the 'typical' or 'average' boy or girl, neither of whom exists in the real world.

This Pocketbook will help you to go beyond the stereotypes to gain a deeper understanding of how gender issues affect two crucial aspects of a teacher's job:

- How you connect with girls and boys
- How you handle your authority with boys and girls

Foreword

Much of the literature in recent years has focused on 'the problem with boys'. The papers have been full of stories about boys falling behind girls in academic achievement, even in so called boy-friendly subjects.

The fact that boys are slower to develop impulse control than girls, find sitting still difficult, and tend to develop language skills later than girls can make them more vulnerable than girls. It has led to a plethora of books about bringing the best out of boys and even to suggestions that boys should start school later than girls.

But focusing on boys as being a problem does not help boys. And it can take the attention away from girls, whose problems in school can be less obvious.

That's why this book focuses on using the same strategies in different ways to motivate boys and girls.

Gender, Motivation and Learning

 Connecting with Boys and Girls

 Being in Control for Boys and Girls

 Involving Boys and Girls in their Learning

 Giving Boys and Girls Effective Feedback

 Separate or Together?

Gender, Motivation and Learning

Boys and girls have same basic needs

All of us – girls and boys, men and women – have the same basic psychological needs. Our motivation comes from our desire to have these needs met. Over the centuries we have become clearer about what these needs are. We now recognise that human beings have three separate, but inter-connected needs.

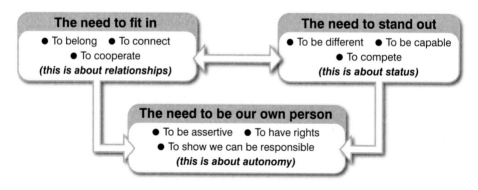

The need to fit in
- To belong ● To connect
- To cooperate
(this is about relationships)

The need to stand out
- To be different ● To be capable
- To compete
(this is about status)

The need to be our own person
- To be assertive ● To have rights
- To show we can be responsible
(this is about autonomy)

Girls tend to have a stronger need than boys to belong

In our society girls have been socialised **to put their need to fit in before their need to stand out**. This can reinforce stereotypical views and hold girls' autonomy in check, leading to girls putting other people's needs before their own and to being passive, pleasing others at their own expense.

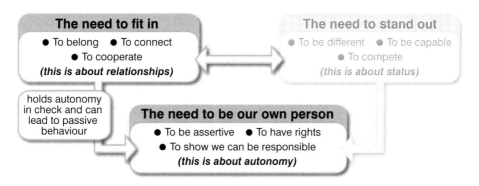

The need to fit in
- To belong   ● To connect
- To cooperate
(this is about relationships)

The need to stand out
- To be different   ● To be capable
- To compete
(this is about status)

holds autonomy in check and can lead to passive behaviour

The need to be our own person
- To be assertive   ● To have rights
- To show we can be responsible
(this is about autonomy)

Boys tend to have a stronger need than girls to stand out

In our society boys have been socialised **to put their need to stand out before their need to fit in**. This can reinforce stereotypical views and drive boys to seek autonomy too fast and lead to aggressive and even violent behaviour.

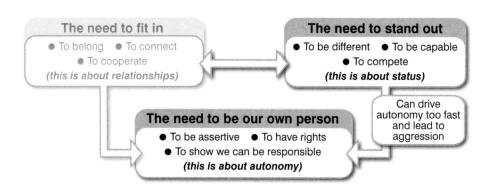

The need to fit in
- To belong   • To connect
- To cooperate
(this is about relationships)

The need to stand out
- To be different   • To be capable
- To compete
(this is about status)

Can drive autonomy too fast and lead to aggression

The need to be our own person
- To be assertive   • To have rights
- To show we can be responsible
(this is about autonomy)

Being your own person

All young people have a strong need to be their own person. This is what psychologists call autonomy and it is about socialisation. It is about feeling able to fit in and stand out.

It is not about independence. It is not about being your own person at the expense of others. It is about having rights and responsibilities, about being trusted and trustworthy. It is about asserting your rights and respecting the rights of others. It is essential in a democratic society.

This need for autonomy applies equally strongly to boys and girls. Where it is not met it can lead to a range of negative reactions: apathy, acquiescence or anger. These not only get in the way of learning but undermine relationships.

The need to be our own person
- To be assertive   ● To have rights
- To show we can be responsible
(this is about autonomy)

A dance between nature and nurture

Gender differences begin to emerge at around the age of two but there is an ongoing debate about where these gender differences come from. Recent research suggests that some of the basic gender differences are present so early that cultural differences cannot be the only cause.

But there are few large scale differences between boys and girls in brain structure or function. It may be that only 3% of the difference in verbal ability between boys and girls is in-born. And although boys seem to be hard-wired for action, 30% of girls are more active than the average boy.

The thinking is that a dance between nature and nurture in the early years of our lives determines what mix of male or female characteristics our brains have.

Male brain, female brain

Psychologist Simon Baron-Cohen talks about the male systematising brain and the female empathising brain* and describes their characteristics:

The male 'systematising' brain

- Hard-wired for understanding and building systems
- Good at analysing, exploring and constructing a system
- Wants to figure out how things work
- Gives you control of the system

The female 'empathising' brain

- Hard-wired for empathy
- Good at identifying and responding to another person's emotions and thoughts
- Wants to connect with other people
- Builds relationships

*The Essential Difference: Men, Women and the Extreme Male Brain. Published by Allen Lane, 2003

Different playground behaviours

Gender differences in behaviour manifest themselves very early on in the playground. Boys tend to play different kinds of games from girls and they tend to relate to each other differently: boys tend to be more hierarchical, girls more collaborative.

Boys

- Boys play power games where dominance and hierarchy are pervasive
- Friendships centre around physical activity and competition
- Most games are competitive with clear cut goals, roles and rules
- The stress in talk is on strategies to reach goals

Girls

- Girls play games in small groups or pairs
- Favourite games don't have clear-cut goals, rules or roles
- What is important in games is the process of interaction
- The stress in talk is on cooperation, collaboration and sensitivity to others' feelings

Different classroom behaviours

In the classroom, meanwhile, girls tend to be better able to articulate their feelings but boys tend to answer in class more often.

Boys
- Boys often want to work but don't know how or are badly organised
- Boys are more noisy in class: they often play the system and disrupt weak teachers
- Boys are academically overconfident and overestimate their abilities
- Boys tend to answer in class more, even when they don't know the right answer
- Boys often pretend to be clever or that they haven't done their homework when they have
- Boys tend to act first and think later: they volunteer first for practical activities

Girls
- Girls tend to be able to plan and organise their work more effectively than boys
- Girls tend to be less disruptive in class, finding ways to kick against the system without getting into trouble
- Girls often underestimate their own abilities
- Girls answer less in class, but they are more likely to ask for help when they need it
- Girls are prepared to be more open about their aspirations than boys
- Girls like to think first and act later: they are slower to become involved in practical activities than boys

Different strengths

Gender differences also manifest themselves in terms of some skills and abilities. But major gender differences seem to lie in patterns of ability rather than in overall level of intelligence.

	Boys	Girls
Word smart	Boys are not so fluent early on. They tend to catch up with girls but never overtake them.	Girls tend to talk earlier and more fluently than boys and written language comes more easily to them.
Logic smart	Boys do better on tests of mathematical reasoning: they are better in the areas of maths that involve abstract concepts and they tend to be analytical.	Girls do better than boys on calculation tests: girls are better at seeing the big picture – they are concerned with context.
Body smart	Boys tend to be more physically active than girls moving faster and staying in motion longer.	Girls develop impulse control quicker than boys.

Given the importance of language in schooling and of sitting still in school, it's not surprising that there have been growing concerns about boys' achievement over the past twenty years.

Different conversations

Linguist Deborah Tannen has spent her working life studying the different ways in which men and women, boys and girls, communicate. Tannen believes that this is what lies behind a great deal of misunderstanding and miscommunication between the genders.

One of the fundamental messages that runs through this Pocketbook is that classrooms are shaped by **the language a teacher uses** in conversations with students, particularly in whole class situations.

The words that we use not only convey information – the message – but, along with our tone of voice and our body language, they also communicate what we are feeling. This is what linguists call the metamessages. See the *Effective Classroom Communication Pocketbook* (details on page 126) for more on this topic.

Being aware of the metamessages we are sending (and being able to read those our pupils are sending us) is critically important in teaching. It can allow us to stop and remind ourselves that others may not mean what we heard them say. Equally, it helps us to be aware that we may be saying one thing but coming across very differently.

Girls and boys need support and challenge

If we want boys and girls to become confident learners we need to help them play to their strengths and tackle their weaknesses. If girls and boys do not have their basic needs met in schools and classrooms they will not learn effectively. To help them meet these needs and be self-motivated learners, boys and girls need the same basic approach from their teachers: a combination of **challenge** and **support**.

The remainder of this Pocketbook is structured around four practical ways in which teachers can provide this combination for both boys and girls:

1. By **connecting** with boys and girls/showing boys and girls that you care
2. By creating a **structured environment** for girls and boys/showing you **trust** them
3. By **actively involving** boys and girls in their own learning/showing you **enjoy teaching** them
4. By giving girls and boys **effective feedback**/showing you **believe in them**

However, as the next sections show, teachers may need to support and challenge girls and boys in different ways.

Gender, Motivation and Learning

 Connecting with Boys and Girls ◄

 Being in Control for Boys and Girls

 Involving Boys and Girls in their Learning

 Giving Boys and Girls Effective Feedback

 Separate or Together?

Connecting with Boys and Girls

Boys and girls want teachers who care

Teaching is a caring profession. When girls and boys are asked what makes a good teacher, relationships are high on their list. In their own words they want teachers who:

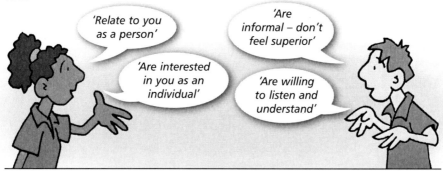

'Relate to you as a person'

'Are informal – don't feel superior'

'Are interested in you as an individual'

'Are willing to listen and understand'

Although boys and girls have the same basic needs, the way they engage with teachers, especially in adolescence, can be very different. You can use this section to reflect on how you show both girls and boys that you care.

Girls have a need to fit in … so do boys

closeness · **connection** · distance

In the previous section we saw that girls have a particular need to feel close to other people and this affects how they behave and how they communicate both in the home, the playground and the classroom.

Linguist Deborah Tannen's work shows that conversation is central to girls' friendships at every age. Girls tend to use the language of cooperation and consideration. They tend to be more collaborative in discussions, supporting each other and developing ideas together. But too much connection, especially in the teenage years, can lead girls as well as boys to feel smothered, suffocated and overwhelmed.

Macho stereotypes suggest that boys will be more distant but one of the greatest paradoxes with boys is that emotional engagement with the lesson and with the teacher is of paramount importance to them. However, you need to engage with boys in a different way than you engage with girls.

We teach who we are

Connecting effectively with other people is not simply about developing a set of skills. It depends on the attitude we hold towards the person we are communicating with. How effectively a teacher connects with a student or a class depends on the basic attitude the teacher holds towards that student or class, not simply the techniques the teacher uses. In this sense we teach who we are.

A teacher who has good people skills but lacks the basic attitudes that promote effective communication with young people will find that their expertise is irrelevant or even harmful, because they will come across as false or manipulative. Pupils are professional teacher-watchers and can see through anything that seems false. So connecting with boys and girls is about self-awareness as well as about developing appropriate people skills.

Easier to connect with boys or girls?

Teachers sometimes say that they feel they relate better to pupils of the same gender as themselves, or to those of the opposite gender. Others believe that it makes no difference. For example, both male and female teachers can find naughty boys an enjoyable challenge, even though they are difficult to teach.

The gender differences in the way that boys and girls connect to teachers, particularly as they grow older, might affect how you relate to young people of the same or opposite gender to yourself.

Boys are less likely to follow the teacher's example, preferring to do it their own way. Boys are not supposed to be too friendly with teachers. Boys can be direct. They tend to act and speak in simple terms. They may not be terribly concerned with pleasing others, especially teachers.

Girls are more concerned than boys with pleasing the teacher and more likely than boys to follow the teacher's example. For them, a close relationship with the teacher can raise their status amongst their peers. They expect the teacher to be on their side, to be an ally. Unlike boys, they tend to ask the teacher for help when they need it.

As you read this section, reflect on whether you find it easier to connect with boys or girls.

Three communication essentials

So what are the essentials of effective communication? The remainder of this section explores the three attitudes or qualities that underpin effective communication in relation to teaching boys and girls.

These are:

1 **Genuineness – what you see is what you get**. (Pages 27-32.)
This means being open and honest about your feelings, asserting your needs and sharing what you really think and believe. It means being who you really are without front or façade.

2 **Respect – unconditional positive regard**. (Pages 33-38.)
This means seeing another person as a fellow human being, who you can accept as a person even though you may not approve of their behaviour.

3 **Empathy – putting yourself in another person's shoes**. (Pages 39-42.)
This means really seeing and hearing another person and understanding that person from their perspective.

1 Be genuine

Being genuine can be risky

No-one is completely genuine and open. All of us play roles, especially in our working lives. Teaching, especially, is like being on stage and beginner teachers are advised to be 'in role' from the very first time they meet a new class, eg:

> *'No matter what you actually feel, show no fear'*
> *'Hide any vulnerability'*
> *'Be relentlessly calm and certain of what you want'*
> *'Remain steadfastly positive and enthusiastic'*

Beginner teachers are also told not to give away too much information about their private lives. Sound advice but difficult to follow. In the early years young children want to know everything about their teacher. As they grow older, students learn not to be over inquisitive, but pupils – no matter what their age or gender – are fascinated to know about their teachers as people and will ask teachers questions about their private lives if they think they can get away with it.

① Be genuine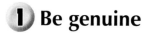

But pupils connect with teachers who are genuine

The advice about playing a role is good advice, but both boys and girls report that they like teachers who are open with them. They say that the best teachers come out from behind their role and – at times and in an appropriate manner – share a bit of themselves while avoiding over-familiarity.

Pupils say they respect teachers who tell you when they are having a bad day, who talk about their own thoughts and feelings and listen to yours, who come across as real people.

If you never come out from behind your role and never feel you can be open and honest about your own feelings, needs and ideas, then it will be impossible to connect closely with your students, whether they are boys or girls.

❶ Be genuine

Look for times when you can be genuine

When you can, be ready for pupils: greet them on arrival and take some time to have a chat with one or two students as they get ready for the lesson. During a lesson, when appropriate and relevant, talk about direct experiences you have had, your thoughts and feelings. This can encourage both girls and boys to do the same, though boys may need more encouragement.

Stop the lesson five minutes early and choose debrief questions that get pupils to share their feelings as well as their thoughts on the lesson, and share a few of your own.

Take time to talk to students around the school, in corridors and the playground.

❶ Be genuine

Admit your mistakes

Say, *'You are right, I agree; I made a mistake'*.

Hypocrisy drives teenagers crazy (and greatly diminishes your authority). When students' criticism is true or accurate, agree with them. It increases your standing and helps you build your relationships with both boys and girls.

Students know better than anyone the pressures that teachers can be under in the classroom. If you feel you have over-reacted be prepared to apologise later if a chance become available.

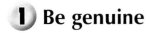 Be genuine

Are you able to get on and off your high horse?

Teachers who get on with young people of both genders know when it is appropriate to drop their role and know how to do it, even with challenging classes. Consider if, when, and how you do that. Can you do it with both boys and girls?

Sometimes playing a role in class can become a kind of ritual or game that works with young people of both genders. For example, it is often said that a good teacher is someone who can 'get on and off their high horse easily'. These teachers pretend to 'get on their high horse' and the pupils accept the game/ritual as real and toe the line. As a result, the teacher then finds it easy to climb off the high horse and things once again proceed smoothly.

1 Be genuine

When in role be a method actor

A class is not a temporary theatre audience willing to suspend disbelief for a couple of hours. Boys and girls are full time teacher-watchers and are remarkably good at figuring out what kind of people teachers really are. That is why what the psychologists call 'surface acting' does not work in the classroom. Teachers need, at times, to be like method actors employing deep acting.

Surface acting	Deep acting
This is when you pretend to feel what you do not actually feel by, for example, forcing a smile or pretending to be angry.	This is when you actually feel the required emotion by, for example, imagining yourself to be in the other person's shoes.
It takes less effort than deep acting but is more likely to lead to stress and emotional exhaustion.	Although it takes a greater level of effort than surface acting, it can make you feel better.
It may work in a brief encounter with a customer from behind a counter but not in a classroom.	It leads to more positive reactions from other people because they understand that you are trying to see their point of view.

2 Be respectful

> *'A boss demands respect; a leader gives it.'* John Adair

Respect can be described as behaviour that makes others feel they are important, worthwhile and special in some way. Every one of us wants respect but we cannot demand it from other people.

Good teachers recognise that the way to get respect is to give it.

To respect someone does not mean that you have to like them or approve of their behaviour, but that you wish and seek their good.

All young people want respect but 'respect' is a word that boys and young men relate to very strongly. Perhaps because of boys' love of hierarchy and need to fit in, feeling disrespected or 'dissed' can lead to aggression and violence.

2 Be respectful

Listen to young people as you listen to adults

Listening is a key way to show respect for and to connect with another person, yet the experience of many girls and boys is that adults don't really listen to them and are more interested in controlling them than finding out who they are and what they have to say.

Listen to young people's views, take them seriously and be open to persuasion. Later we'll look at the importance of constructive talk in classrooms (pages 71-78) but first, ask yourself how often in class/individual discussions you go down the '3 levels of listening':

Level 1 – Pretending to listen
You carry on what you are doing, while appearing to give the pupil your attention and occasionally making *'u- uh'* or *'that's nice'* noises.

Level 2 – Selective listening
This is a kind of pretend listening but where you prick up your ears every now and again to select something interesting to respond to.

Level 3 – Active listening
Giving your full and complete attention.

2 Be respectful

Listening and maintaining your point of view

The key thing is to listen while maintaining your own point of view. However, be aware that girls may be too ready to agree with you rather than forming or maintaining their own point of view.

Teenage boys, by contrast, can be full of value judgements and they can be expressed as if they are absolute truths rather than simply opinions. Avoid putting them down; agree with their right to an opinion while maintaining your own point of view.

Give both girls and boys the message that they could be right and why they might think that, but that you have a different point of view.

❷ Be respectful

Listen when emotions are running high

Listening can help calm girls and boys down when they are emotional but you are not sure what they are feeling.

It can help boys and girls to express their emotions and help boys especially to widen their emotional vocabulary (see page 121).

2 Be respectful

Use appropriate body language with boys and girls

We listen with the whole body, not simply our ears. Getting on the same level with both girls and boys will help you to connect with them as well as to listen.

It can be a good idea when you are working with a boy to sit down next to him and spread the materials out in front of you so you are both looking at the materials shoulder to shoulder. This is less confrontational than sitting face to face.

Looking a girl in the eye when you are helping her gives her reassurance that you like her and are on her side. Too many teachers (especially men) don't make eye contact with female students.

Eye contact with a teacher can make boys uncomfortable. Don't hold an eye contact stare with a boy unless you are trying to discipline or reprimand him.

2 Be respectful

Smile

'A smile is the shortest distance between two people.'

In a workshop a science teacher commented, "Last week a girl in my Y9 class said to me: *'Sir, why do you **never** smile?'* I responded immediately with a tongue-in-cheek remark: *'Chemistry is no laughing matter'*. But when I went away and thought about it I realised that she was right."

His question was what should he do about it? He pointed out that there were teachers in his school who were brilliant stand-up comedians, but he wasn't one of them. He was reminded that there are lots of occasions when you can smile apart from when someone has cracked a joke.

3 Be empathetic

Empathy lies between apathy and sympathy. It is what young people growing up in a rapidly changing world need. They will connect with adults who show that they are trying to understand how difficult this is for them.

But young people don't want our sympathy nor will they connect with adults who appear not to care.

Apathy
Behaviour that shows you have a lack of feeling or concern for another person.

'I don't care how you feel.'

Empathy
Behaviour that shows you have some knowledge of another person's world as they are experiencing it.

'I am trying to understand how you must feel.'

Sympathy
Behaviour that shows you want to share the feelings of another person.

'I know how you feel.'

3 Be empathetic

Take an interest in girls and boys as people

You can show empathy by taking an interest in boys and girls as people and in acknowledging young people's view of the world.

Make an effort to learn and use the names of all your students and show an interest in boys' and girls' opinions, their likes and dislikes, what they are interested in. Find out about their hobbies and special interests. Do they have any brothers or sisters?

If you teach teenagers, it's worthwhile keeping up to some extent with the current music, fashion or football scenes. It helps, for example, when you know that the majority of the boys in your class support a particular football team that lost a key match last night to be able to say: *'I hear it didn't go well last night'*.

Acknowledgement doesn't mean approval but it does demonstrate a desire to stay in touch with what interests and concerns girls and boys.

3 Be empathetic

Use open questions with boys of few words

Unfortunately, a chat with boys of few words can easily turn into an interrogation.

Try avoiding closed questions such as *Who? What? Where? When?* that lend themselves to single word or short answers.

Use more open questions that start with *Which? How?* and *Why?* They are invitations to tell you about something.

But beware of questions that are too open or broad in scope – like, *'How is it going?'* or, *'What have you been up to lately?'* These tend to elicit answers such as, 'Pretty good', 'Not bad' or 'Not a lot'. The key is to find an area of mutual interest and only ask these questions when you genuinely want to hear what the other person has to say.

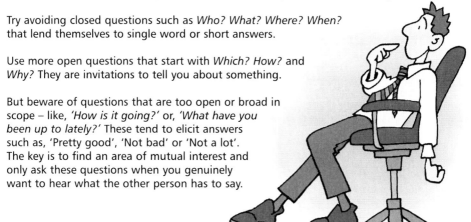

3 Be empathetic

Inject some humour

It has been said that laughter prevents 'a hardening of the attitudes' and can be a good way to defuse a confrontation. There is overwhelming evidence to suggest that humour helps us to lead happier, healthier, longer lives. It also helps us to learn. If you want to inject more humour into your classroom, the following is good advice:

- Ask yourself *'what makes **me** laugh?'*
- Make sure all humour is appropriate, timely and tasteful
- Be particularly vigilant about jokes that are made at a pupil's expense
- Be willing to laugh at yourself and help pupils gain confidence to laugh at themselves
- Begin with gradual and low-risk humour

Boys are often mischievous and they like the rude and the ridiculous. However, their humour is often seen as inappropriate, immature and disruptive – something to be suppressed rather than channelled.

Both boys and girls will use their intellect to clown around and make lessons fun by engaging in off-task behaviour. Try to respond to humour playfully by assuming a playful intent, not taking it personally, and encouraging all to laugh and then move on.

Gender, Motivation and Learning

 Connecting with Boys and Girls

 Being in Control for Boys and Girls

 Involving Boys and Girls in their Learning

 Giving Boys and Girls Effective Feedback

 Separate or Together?

Being in Control for Boys and Girls

Boys and girls want teachers who set limits

A lot has been written about boys' need for structure, but girls need this too. Both girls and boys have little time for teachers who cannot control a class; they need to feel that they are in a safe and secure environment.

Boys and girls want teachers whom they can trust to create this kind of environment, by:

'Letting you know where you stand.'

'Being firm and fair.'

However, they also want teachers to be assertive rather than authoritarian, who:

'Don't boss you about.'

'Are strict for you not for themselves.'

'Share their power.'

Use the next page and the rest of this section to reflect on whether you:
- Seek to manage boys' and girls' behaviour differently
- Are more protective of girls and more repressive of boys
- Find it harder to give boys or girls autonomy

Do you treat boys and girls differently?

Researchers report that few teachers acknowledge or recognise that they treat girls and boys *significantly* differently in the normal course of classroom teaching. They think that they themselves would notice or be aware if they did. Only a few teachers admit that their perceptions may not be the reality.

In interviews with pupils it's easy for the following stereotypes to emerge:

What girls say	What boys say
'We are treated more like adults and boys are treated more like children.'	'Girls get away with a lot more than boys.'
'We are expected to be better behaved than boys.'	'Boys are blamed for everything.'
'Boys play up in lessons.'	'Girls can get away with not doing the work by keeping quiet.'
'Boys get more attention because of their bad behaviour.'	'We find it difficult to sit down for long whereas the girls are used to it.'

Boys and girls want to know where they stand

hierarchy **control** equality

Classrooms are hierarchical and, as teachers, we need to be in control without putting young people down. This is particularly important for boys. They need to know where they stand with other people and where they fit in the hierarchy, but we **all** need structure in our lives. Without structure we feel uncertain and insecure.

Both boys and girls dislike structures that are unclear or contradictory. Both are strong believers in rules and discipline. Younger children want a safe and secure environment; older students want to know where they stand. Students usually suggest there should be more and stricter rules, not fewer. Among the teachers they most dislike are those whom they say 'can't' or 'won't' control their classes.

Boys more likely to challenge

As we've seen, boys tend to have a greater need to know where they stand in the pecking order than girls. This can lead them to being more likely than girls to challenge the teacher's authority openly and push for autonomy too hard and too soon.

Consequently, boys appear to have a greater need for structure than girls. If the teacher doesn't take charge, they begin to compete with each other to establish the pecking order, with some going on the offensive and others being forced onto the defensive.

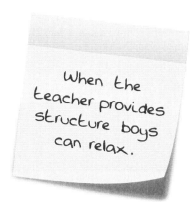

When the teacher provides structure boys can relax.

'Boys need strong discipline' is a myth

The idea of boys needing 'strong discipline' is a myth. Boys may want structure but they don't want teachers who are punitive.

Boys can be more emotionally fragile than girls. A lot of boys' aggressive behaviour can be instigated by girls or by another boy's verbal aggression.

Humiliating a boy in front of his classmates is not a good idea. Dressing down a boy in front of others may work in the short term but boys will react by spending a lot of time being resentful and angry and looking for ways to get even. The balance to strike with boys is between reminding them of their responsibilities to work with others while meeting their desire for autonomy, eg:

> *'Tim, I can see you were really keen to get going there, but sometimes it's important to hold back... to be a team player.'*

Girls less likely to challenge teacher authority

We've seen how girls tend to be more cooperative than boys and more anxious to fit in than to stand out. They hold their autonomy in check and seek to please others at their own expense. This can lead to girls being less likely than boys to openly challenge the teacher's authority.

As a result, girls might appear to have less need for structure than boys. But this, too, is a myth. Just like boys, girls want to know where they stand. Like boys, they do not respect teachers who don't provide structure.

If the teacher does not take charge girls are less likely than boys to go on the offensive but will still seek to establish a pecking order, with some being manipulative and others going on the defensive.

When the teacher provides structure girls can relax.

Girls want autonomy too

The great danger for girls is that because they appear to be more biddable than boys teachers mistakenly think that they don't want autonomy or are not capable of being autonomous. Instead of challenging girls to take more responsibility and to be more autonomous, teachers can collude with girls who hold their autonomy in check and take advantage of their passive behaviour.

Think back to the diagram on page 10. Girls and boys can give themselves **affiliation** by making friends, and they can give themselves **status** by doing something that their classmates admire. But young people cannot award themselves **autonomy** – neither in the school nor the home. Autonomy is generated within a power relationship.

So how we can satisfy both boys' and girls' need for autonomy?

Our reluctance to grant autonomy

From the time they are born to their teenage years boys and girls have a growing need to be autonomous. This, along with adults' reluctance to grant them autonomy, is perhaps the most important issue in motivating both boys and girls in school.

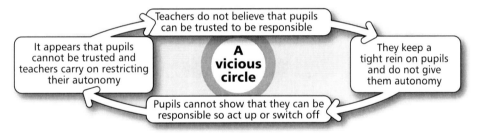

Both boys and girls need to learn how to earn autonomy within a healthy power relationship. How adults can help them to do this is a central theme of this Pocketbook.

Starting with some don'ts (pages 52-56), the rest of this section deals with ways of helping young people to become autonomous.

Avoid the 'teacher as boss' approach

The 'teacher as boss' approach leads to restricted autonomy and does not help boys or girls to become independent learners. This style is usually accompanied by aggression, which undermines relationships, makes enemies, and builds up resentment in both boys and girls.

Boys may be more likely to become antagonistic and respond with anger, hostility and belligerence than girls. Girls may be more likely than boys to be devious or to acquiesce, to feel cowed or submissive.

Avoid 'a good talking to'

Classrooms can be stressful places and when we're dealing with conflict in the classroom we sometimes become aggressive and slip into patterns of speech which are actually barriers to communication.

Which of the following do you slip into using? Are there some you would use with boys and not girls or vice versa?

Giving orders:	*'Be quiet!'; 'Sit up in your seat!'*
Threatening:	*'See me at the end of the lesson.'* *'I don't want to have to tell you again.'*
Being dismissive:	*'This work is simply not good enough!'* *'That won't work!'*
Moralising:	*'You ought to be ashamed of yourself!'*
Giving heavy-handed advice:	*'You need to get your act together!'*
Excessive questioning:	*'Where have you been?'*

Don't shout at boys or plead with girls

Boys hate being yelled at, but some teachers think that boys don't suffer as a result of it as much as girls. In reality many boys are lightning conductors for harsh discipline, much more so than girls.

Use 'please' and 'thank you' with boys and girls, ensuring that your tone of voice when saying please does not communicate to boys that you are 'soft' or to girls that you are pleading.

When we speak in a courteous way we show an interest in others, respect for their importance and care for their feelings. We are teaching them that politeness builds relationships.

Avoid passive behaviour

Being passive does not help young people to be autonomous. When we behave passively we don't stand up for our rights, appearing instead just to accept the treatment meted out to us by others. We:

- Over apologise
- Put ourselves down
- Are unclear or rambling
- Dismiss our own needs
- Do not state clearly what we think or feel

Neither boys nor girls have respect for a teacher who avoids controlling pupils and who relies instead on them being self-disciplined and self-motivated. Aggressive boys or manipulative girls will take the lead in the class and treat the teacher with contempt.

Passivity on behalf of the teacher leads to many girls and boys feeling anxious, insecure or frustrated. Some girls or boys may take pity on the teacher, but whatever affection they have for that teacher will soon grow cold.

Avoid manipulative behaviour

Manipulative behaviour is harder to spot and define, but being manipulative does not help young people to be autonomous. It can be about arranging things so that they come out the way you want. If this benefits the class it's acceptable but it is often indirect aggression such as:

- Flattering people so that they will do what we want
- Making excuses for not doing things
- Off-loading blame for your mistakes onto others
- Sarcastic remarks or put downs where your meaning isn't entirely clear

This kind of manipulation is counterproductive; it damages pupils' respect and their trust in you.

Be assertive

Being assertive is the only way to help young people become autonomous. Assertiveness is the clear, honest and direct communication of positive and negative feelings and opinions while at the same time respecting the rights, feelings and opinions of others. It is the kind of behaviour we want our young people to adopt and so they need to see it modelled by teachers in the classroom.

People find it challenging to receive assertive messages. Boys and girls can respond to assertive messages with aggressive or passive behaviour.

Learning to be assertive is a lifelong journey for most of us as we have been trained to be passive by parents and teachers. None of us can be assertive all the time. In stressful situations we all end up sometimes being authoritarian or passive.

Six assertiveness skills

Here are the six basic skills of assertiveness to use when raising a matter of concern with someone. Reflect on how effectively you use these skills with both boys and girls.

1 Know what you want to achieve before you engage with the pupil.

2 Be direct and straight to the point – don't beat about the bush.

3 Be clear what specific change you want and state it.

4 Describe the behaviour, not the person.

5 Listen empathetically to what they say in response.

6 Do not be sidetracked by something you think is irrelevant or get into a discussion.

Being assertive in itself is not enough to maintain discipline in a classroom. We all need an effective behaviour management system to deal with the indiscipline that will occur no matter how effectively we are able to be assertive. We have to adopt a staged approach to giving boys and girls autonomy, within limits.

Take a staged approach to autonomy

Effective, assertive teachers recognise that when they discipline boys and girls they have short-term goals: to prevent disruptive behaviour and create order in the classroom for instance. But they also have long-term goals, which in fact are the most important goals but can be forgotten in the heat of the moment: they want to work with boys and girls who are self-regulating and self-motivated.

Effective teachers start by imposing their authority and establishing **a secure classroom**. When they judge a class is ready, they let go of the reins and move into a **sharing classroom** and then finally into a **self-motivating classroom**. How you can emulate this is the theme of the rest of this section.

3 **The self-motivating classroom:** allowing a measure of self determination

2 **The sharing classroom:** encouraging and enabling pupil autonomy

1 **The secure classroom:** setting clear limits

Stage 1 Establishing a secure classroom

When establishing a secure classroom the aim is to develop self-discipline by being authoritative, assertive and fair, giving conditional support and focusing on conformity and correction. At this stage:

- You will set clear and possible goals for students
- There are a few rules which are explicit and clear
- Your responses to infringements are predictable
- Learning is directed and the outcome usually predictable
- You use praise and extrinsic rewards

The pupils are motivated to learn because they feel they ought to or should. They are involved in activities that interest and engage them and they respect their teacher, believe he/she cares about their progress and gives them effective support.

A. State your expectations explicitly and positively

If you say *'don't be late'*, *'don't call out'*, *'messing around again!'* then pupils will interpret these as *'I expect you to be late'*, *'I expect you to call out'*, *'I expect you to mess about,'* and if that's what you expect of them then that is how they will be.

Instead of   *'Don't be late'*

try: **'I expect everyone to be sitting in their places by two o'clock'**

Instead of   *'Don't call out'*

say: **'Put your hand up, then I can listen to what you have to say'**

Instead of   *'Messing around again!'*

say: **'I expect you to work quietly until the bell goes'**

B. Use inclusive language

Teaching can be very much a 'you and them' situation. A way of changing this is to use inclusive language, making more use of the word *'we'* and less use of the words *'I'* and *'you'*. For example:

'We don't put our feet on the seats here.'

'We are working well today.'

This is the language of connection and relationships rather than the language of power and authority.

C. Establish non-negotiable rights and responsibilities

Pupils know that schools give teachers power to establish secure classrooms, but it is helpful for them to hear that you plan to use that power to guarantee their rights. Make it clear from the start that everyone in the class has:

- The right to feel safe
- The right to learn
- The right to be treated with respect

Point out that our rights come with the responsibility not to infringe on other people's rights. We have the responsibility to consider and respect other people's rights. You may want to add here that you can't *make* them learn and you can't do the learning for them.

D. The classroom contract

It's worth agreeing a classroom contract based on rights and responsibilities. The contract model is powerful for three reasons:

1. It rests on a foundation of everyone's right to learn.
2. The rules are not imposed abstractions: students discuss and define what the rules will look like in reality.
3. Students know that everybody will have to abide by the rules.

Very young children have an emerging concept of 'rightness' that can be drawn upon to develop this kind of classroom agreement or contract. The idea of a 'full value contract' appears in a range of collaborative learning programmes – a social contract agreed upon with the class to create a 'safe place to be'. Teachers provide moral leadership by positing some guiding rights (like those on the previous page) and principles (like those below) around which specific rules and expectations can be developed. For example, what it means for a group to:

- Play safe
- Play hard
- Play fair

E. From punishments to consequences

Rules will always be broken and need to be enforced, but punishments can be problematic with both boys and girls.

Some boys see punishments as confirming their status with their peers. Others will make out that punishments don't hurt them.

Getting into trouble generally doesn't play so well in female groups but girls can be humiliated by punishment and can be tempted to get their own back by gossiping or making fun of a teacher behind their back.

It's best for a teacher to think in terms of consequences rather than punishments. This helps both boys and girls link their disruptive or wrong behaviour to an outcome which emphasises fairness and justice and hopefully encourages a sense of responsibility. For example, staying behind after class and clearing up their mess.

F. Avoid sharing power too quickly

Give whatever time it takes to establish a secure classroom. It won't all be plain sailing:

- Boys may act up in ways that would previously have been suppressed in an authoritarian classroom
- Girls may not take part in discussions or play dumb when asked directly to offer suggestions
- Boys may say that it's the teacher's job to make decisions and rules, not the students'
- Girls may simply tell you what they think you want to hear
- Both boys and girls may welcome the chance to take decisions, take it seriously, but come up with a bad decision

It takes time and persistence with difficult classes to win the trust and respect of pupils. If you persist they will come to admire you for it.

Stage 2 Moving on to a sharing classroom

During the second stage of the move to enabling pupil autonomy, your aim is to develop students' self-confidence by emphasising trust and accountability, by having positive expectations and by being an encouraging adult.

In a sharing classroom, rules are negotiated and there is a focus on progress. Goal-setting is a process shared with students and students are challenged to the limits of their ability. Learning outcomes are negotiated and there is opportunity for curiosity and enjoyment. As the teacher, you go beyond praise and rewards to encouragement. Boys and girls are motivated to learn because they admire their teacher whom they believe empowers them and helps them to bring out the best in themselves.

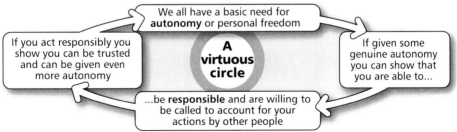

We all have a basic need for **autonomy** or personal freedom

A virtuous circle

If given some genuine autonomy you can show that you are able to...

...be **responsible** and are willing to be called to account for your actions by other people

If you act responsibly you show you can be trusted and can be given even more autonomy

Stage 3 The self-motivating classroom

In stage three of the process, your aim is to develop self-motivation by empowering students and affirming them. As their teacher, you know your pupils well and value them. Pupils feel responsible for their own successes and progress:

- They have autonomy: they set their own goals with help
- Students are self-regulating: they devise and keep their own rules
- There is 'flow': students are involved in open-ended problem-solving, decision-making and creative thinking

There is the discipline of community characterised by *'You do it because this is the way we do things around here: this is the nature of the agreements, customs and rules that bind us together'*.

It's worth remembering that when teachers aspire to become more democratic, they may be yielding **power**, but they should never yield **authority**. When teachers confuse power and authority, they become less assertive and the transition fails.

Gender,
Motivation
and Learning

 Connecting
with Boys
and Girls

 Being in
Control for
Boys and Girls

 Involving Boys
and Girls in
their Learning

 Giving Boys and
Girls Effective
Feedback

 Separate or
Together?

Involving Boys
and Girls in
their Learning

Make learning interesting

In the last chapter we looked at how girls' and boys' need for autonomy can be met in the way a classroom is run. This chapter looks at how it can be met by actively involving them in their own learning.

Teachers often point out that pupils don't want to be active learners, and can't or won't think for themselves. But both girls and boys soon switch off or 'act up' if the classroom is not a stimulating environment and they aren't actively involved in their own learning.

When pupils are asked what makes a good teacher they talk about teachers who challenge, who help them to think and learn for themselves and, crucially, who enjoy teaching them. Girls and boys want teachers who:

Constructive talk

Constructive talk is an essential ingredient of a good lesson. We learn by having conversations: conversations in our heads and conversations with other people. These help us to make sense of what we are learning and to apply it in different situations.

Conversation also involves pupils in their learning and can transform relationships in the classroom. Talk allows pupils to express their doubts, clarifies their understanding and helps them share their feelings, thoughts and preferences. It can help the teacher to relax and bring pleasure and fun into the classroom.

Constructive talk may be important but it can be hard to handle in challenging classrooms. As a result teachers are tempted to close conversations down or keep talk under strict control.

The gender factor in class discussion

Encouraging all pupils to contribute productively is one of the difficulties with classroom discussion. Extroversion and introversion have a big impact on who contributes: extroverted girls are more likely to contribute than introverted boys. But gender is also a factor.

Boys and girls have different conversational styles as the next two pages show. If, like the vast majority of teachers in the UK, you teach mixed gender classes, you can use these pages to reflect on the extent to which these differences show up in your classroom. You can also use them to reflect on how you handle gender issues in whole-class discussions and what changes you might consider making.

Most teachers claim they are gender neutral but when it comes to class discussions, the research can tell a different story. For example, one study* showed that teachers can be up to four times less likely to ask higher order questions of girls than of boys.

*Boys, Girls and Achievement by Becky Francis. Publisher, Routledge, 2000

Boys' conversational style

Boys tend to use speech to attract and maintain an audience and assert a position of dominance. They tend to be more competitive in discussions, trying to score points or outdo each other.

Dominant boys are more likely to volunteer comments in class and teachers call on them more frequently. They are also more likely to respond spontaneously, without putting their hands up, and may interrupt when others have the floor. Consequently, they can receive the lion's share of the teacher's attention.

Boys down the pecking order, however, are reluctant to talk in classroom discussions.

All boys become reluctant to talk about how they feel in class discussions much earlier than girls.

Girls' conversational style

Girls are more willing to 'chip in' in class nowadays than they were in the past.

But they can still tend to lose their voice in classroom discussions as they approach adolescence. When they do contribute in class, their interaction style can be different from that of boys.

Girls are more likely than boys to raise their hands than to shout out an answer and are more likely to respond on task. However, they are less likely to raise their hand to ask a question, offer a comment or challenge anyone. They may save these for after class, one-to-one, informally with the teacher. But girls' questions, though less frequent, are often more constructive.

Ensure everyone gets a hearing

The following strategies will help you to ensure that introverts as well as extroverts and girls as well as boys get a hearing in whole-class lessons:

- Using 'wait time' (leaving at least three seconds after you have asked a question before you pick on someone with their hand up to respond) to ensure you have more choice of girls and boys to pick on
- Pick on pupils to answer questions on a strict girl/boy rotation
- Have a no-hands-up policy where you can pick on anyone to respond after wait time

Think, pair and share

It's clear from the previous pages that to help all boys and girls to talk effectively in the classroom teachers need to be skilful in using a mix of whole class, paired and small group discussion. The simplest and most flexible way to do this is to make 'Think, pair and share' a normal routine during lessons.

'Think, pair and share' is an age-old technique for getting children actively involved during a lesson. It helps all pupils to learn by both thinking and talking:

1. Students are asked individually to write down as many answers, ideas or suggestions as they can ('Think').

2. Next they are asked to pool their ideas with a partner ('Pair').

3. Then the teacher opens it up for contributions from the class as a whole ('Share').

Talk partners

A more structured approach than the impromptu 'Think, pair and share' is to have pupils sit with a talk or learning partner with whom they work on short paired tasks built into the lesson. It's a useful strategy for all classes but particularly when class lessons are hard to handle.

Plan short two-minute activities in advance to insert into the lesson, eg:

- Brainstorming an idea
- Drawing a mind map
- Comparing two things
- Ranking statements in an order
- Considering pros and cons
- Making a list
- Recalling an experience in their own life
- Ranking statements as positive/negative/not sure

(Note: for a discussion of the advantages and disadvantages of mixed gender pairs see pages 115-117.)

Group challenges

Moving from pairs to groups of four or more allows boys and girls to experience working as a team. Group challenges can work for girls and boys.

There is a wealth of material to help teachers develop collaborative learning in the classroom, where pupils work together on group challenges to produce a product for a purpose and an audience and by so doing make sense of what they are learning and support each other to learn.

Working in groups enables girls to **cooperate**; it challenges and supports boys to do the same.

If the groups **compete** to produce the best product, then boys are able to compete and girls are supported to do the same.

Boys and girls like what they are good at

'Why are we doing this?' is a question that boys may be more likely to pose than girls, who may be more compliant and willing to please the teacher or have a higher boredom threshold. But both boys and girls tend to become interested and involved in what they are good at, or perhaps what they are socialised to think they should be good at. In the early years this can mean that:

Boys like:
    Action
    Objects
    Doing

Girls like:
    Reading
    Writing
    Talking

At secondary level it can mean that both boys and girls typically think that:

- PE, maths and science (especially physics) are boys' subjects
- Languages, the creative arts, humanities and biology are girls' subjects
- Boys don't like reading but when they do read they prefer non-fiction
- Girls like fiction and stories about relationships

Reading and writing

One of the major reasons boys and girls turn away from school is that they struggle with reading and writing. Both need help to be good at these skills.

Over the past decade the focus has been on boys' problems with literacy. It has been established that compared with the average girl, the average boy:

- Learns to use language later
- Takes longer to read and write
- Values reading and writing less

The reasons for this are difficult to identify. There is no firm evidence indicating whether it's to do with linguistic ability or with how the male brain develops.

Indeed, it may have more to do with socialisation, as what we are coming to recognise is that a large number of girls also turn away from reading and writing between the ages of 8 and 11. This is why the following pages focus on how to actively involve both boys and girls in reading and writing.

Different reading interests

Boys tend to read to find out. They tend to favour non-fiction over fiction: descriptions of real events or illustrated accounts of how things work. Even when boys are reading fiction they want to find out what is going to happen: they focus on the action and the plot. Left to their own devices many boys shy away from fiction altogether.

Girls tend to like dissecting and exploring relationships, analysing characters' motives and behaviours. This is why they tend to enjoy short stories and novels more than boys. The danger for them is that they can become bored or uninterested in reading non-fiction and don't develop the strategies they need to study.

Play to boys' and girls' interests

There is a strong argument for playing to boys' and girls' reading and writing interests, especially in upper primary and secondary school. It's worth talking to them about what these interests are. You may or may not find they coincide with what writers on gender suggest they are:

Girls want to read about
Animals
Mystery
Social conflict
Emotional courage

Boys want to read about
Adventure
Inventions
War
Physical courage

Girls want to write about
Friends and family
What is on my mind
Dreams

Boys want to write about
How to do something
Sport
Action

Beware reinforcing stereotypes

If boys and girls are simply left to choose what they read or are directed towards what are seen to be gender-appropriate books and gender-appropriate writing, there is a danger that stereotypes are reinforced.

It's important to look beyond the stereotypes both in the kinds of topics boys and girls are asked to read and write about and how these topics are actually taught.

For example, both boys and girls like stories about courage, either fictional or real life. They love heroes and heroines. History and fiction give boys and girls an opportunity to explore, understand and value emotional courage. They can then apply the idea to their own circumstances. It takes courage to stand up for someone who is being picked on. The more nervous you are about doing something the more courage it takes to do it.

It's not just what, it's how

It's not just the books you choose, it's also the way you teach them.

In the Harry Potter books, for example, you might appeal to boys' need to be different by asking them to imagine what it would be like to be able to fly. You might appeal to girls' need to connect by asking them which character they identify with most.

Lord of the Flies, which is peopled entirely by male characters, can be considered as a boys' book but girls can be asked questions that explore relationships between the boys, eg: *'How would you feel if you were Piggy?'*

One teacher found that boys simply wanted to rush through the book to find out what happened rather than exploring the relationships between the boys in depth. He asked them to create a 3D map of the island using papier-mâché, cardboard and paint. This physical activity appealed to the boys and forced them to read the book carefully all the way through to the closing chapter.

Helping boys and girls with writing

The following ideas for helping with writing apply to both boys and girls and to all kinds of writing across subject areas:

- Ask them to write first and foremost about what interests them, particularly if they are reluctant or under-confident writers
- Allow boys and girls to produce their first draft without worrying about the mechanics
- Ask boys and girls to polish their best pieces of writing, not every piece
- Give separate grades for the way both boys and girls express their ideas and for the spelling and grammar
- Encourage boys and girls to draw pictures or use graphic organisers before writing

Don't leave reading to chance

It's wise not to leave reading simply to chance, particularly between the ages 8 and 11 when boys' and girls' reading tends to drop off. Some teachers try to split the difference and look for books that appeal to both, but there are few such books, especially in the early years.

Draw up the reading histories (both fiction and non fiction) of individual children at that age so that their reading can be monitored and help given where required, eg:

- Find different ways to approach texts, not simply giving accounts of plots or writing character studies

- Bring fiction and non fiction together on a specific topic (eg wolves) so that pupils can study the topic from different angles

- Ask male and female teachers to talk about books they have enjoyed and why

- Involve the community in recommending books. Players from a local team were invited into one school to recommend reading, including information texts, poetry and a range of fictional genres. These then formed a 'Read the Team List' to read that term

Boys need to move more than girls

Whether it is hard-wired into the male brain or not, all the evidence shows that the average boy needs to move more than the average girl. Movement reduces aggression, decreases boredom and it aids concentration and involvement in learning.

In nursery this is readily understood and learning is physically active. Boys and girls are able to move about, manipulate things and handle objects for a large part of the time. Sitting still and listening is encouraged but only in small doses.

As pupils move up from nursery to primary and primary to secondary, learning becomes increasingly sedentary and the scope for moving, manipulating and handling decreases. Students are increasingly required to sit still for long periods and fidgeting is frowned upon. This can be difficult for girls, but is even more difficult for the average boy. It can lead to discipline problems and boredom.

Build-in movement formally in primary...

The claim that certain kinds of movements cross the lateral in the brain and help link left brain and right brain, and that certain movements help certain kinds of learning is far from proven. However, movement definitely wakes up the brain and keeps it active. At primary level, formally incorporating movement into the day is key.

Brief and simple activities that can be done on the spot and without materials, and that can be sprinkled throughout the day at appropriate times, are ideal. It's best if such activities are not seen as a break from learning but a chance to chill out and recharge.

In addition, it is meat and drink for primary teachers to build movement wherever possible into whatever children are doing, eg:

- Number lines in maths
- Line-ups to sort out groups
- Standing up or staying seated to vote for right/wrong answers

...less formally in secondary

Incorporating movement can be difficult in non-practical classes in secondary, especially if space is limited and the furniture difficult to move around. Also, teenagers aren't into playing 'brain breaks'. Some of the following ideas may be more practical than others:

- Half-way though a period, give the class the chance to stop work, get up and move around. They can sharpen a pencil, socialise, hand in paperwork or just walk around. Give them a set amount of time so they can monitor themselves

- Simply allow pupils to stand and listen for a few moments during a class lesson and then sit down again if they want to

- Manage your classroom tightly to allow all pupils freedom to move around to collect materials or resources and to hand in work, etc

- Have a range of items to handle where possible, eg card sorts, worksheets, whiteboards to write on and hold up, etc

- Give some boys something safe to fidget with, or issue them with doodling pads for listening activities in class or for note-writing

Design activities that require movement

Activities that require movement can be built into any subject, eg:

* Form a line across the class from 'strongly agree' to 'strongly disagree' with 'don't knows' in the middle
* Do 'Think, pair and share' (page 76) walking about with your partner

Or they can be subject specific:

* Form a timeline across the class in history
* Have pupils graph themselves in geography
* Dramatise the life-cycle process in biology
* Make human number-lines in maths

For other ideas along these lines, see the *Drama for Learning Pocketbook* by Brian Radcliffe, Teachers' Pocketbooks, 2007.

Gender, Motivation and Learning

 Connecting with Boys and Girls

 Being in Control for Boys and Girls

 Involving Boys and Girls in their Learning

 Giving Boys and Girls Effective Feedback

 Separate or Together?

Giving Boys and Girls Effective Feedback

Boys and girls want teachers who believe in them

When boys and girls are asked what makes a good teacher they almost always mention the quality of feedback a teacher gives them. They all want teachers who:

'Notice when you are having difficulties'

'Tell you how you are doing'

'Encourage you to do better'

'Help you when you are stuck'

Perhaps the reason both boys and girls put so much emphasis on feedback is that it is the single most important way in which a teacher communicates his or her belief that a young person can grow, learn and develop. You can use this section to monitor how effectively you communicate this belief to both boys and girls.

Boys and girls have different beliefs about ability

US psychologist Carol Dweck has spent most of her working life studying our views about intelligence and specifically to what extent we think intelligence is learned or in-born.

She has found that both boys and girls who think that intelligence is mainly in-born are more likely to give up when they get into difficulties at school. Students with this belief put their difficulties down to the 'fact' that they lack intelligence. They reason that trying harder or using different techniques to help them learn is pointless.

Dweck discovered* that the kind of feedback teachers give can unwittingly reinforce these negative mindsets and that there are differences in the way that boys and girls react when they get into difficulties.

*Self-Theories: Their Role in Motivation, Personality and Development. Psychology Press, 2000

Boys' competitive mindset

Boys tend to have a competitive mindset and are more likely to set competitive goals than girls. For boys, success is about being better than others. They try to be the best or at least to appear smarter or stronger than their peers. They feel pressure to make getting good grades look easy and never get caught working.

Boys set competitive goals and getting good grades tends to be more important to them than they will admit. As a result, they can have unrealistically high expectations of their own academic performance and if they don't think they can compete they may opt out.

Many boys who do not think they are smart or strong are motivated by a fear of failure and will slip into what psychologists call 'self-worth protection'. This can mean that they will spend their time avoiding looking stupid, and when they get poor results pretending they don't care. Or they may set easy goals and if they get B's or C's think they are brilliant.

Feedback may need to give boys a reality check

Boys can be 'over the top'. They may overestimate their own ability and appear not to be greatly influenced by what others think of them or to be arrogant 'know-it-alls'. But this is often a front which masks a sense of insecurity.

It's important to be realistic with boys without putting them down. The trick is to encourage an accurate match between aspirations and skills while ensuring they remain optimistic about their success. For example, the third response below is the best:

Teacher: *'What do you want to do when you grow up?'*
Boy: *'Play for Manchester United!'*

Potential responses:

1 *'Do you really think you will be able to do that?'*

2 *'It might be better to have some other ideas just in case.'*

3 **'What do you think you will have to do to be able to play for them?'**

Girls' mastery mindset

Girls tend to have a mastery mindset. Unlike boys who want to be the best, girls try to do their best, to be all they can be. As a result, they tend to measure success in their own terms and are more able to view grades as a means to an end than boys.

But if girls don't think they can achieve, they may opt out altogether. A belief that intelligence is fixed can be even more damaging for girls than it is for boys. This is true even for girls who are very academic.

Carol Dweck has studied the impact of beliefs about intelligence on girls and has coined the phrase 'bright girls syndrome'. It describes girls who, because they are academically bright, tend to do well at school and put it down to the fact that they have been lucky enough to have been born smart. But at some point they come across something they can't do, no matter how hard they try. They put it down to the fact that they have been 'found out' – they believe they have reached the limits of their intelligence and they crash out.

Feedback may need to encourage and challenge girls

When it comes to aspirations girls tend to be more 'feet on the ground' than boys. Indeed, even very able girls may lack confidence in their own ability and be excessively critical in evaluating their own work and their own performance.

Girls are also more likely to want to please the teacher.

For both these reasons girls can be vulnerable to criticism. A negative comment from a teacher may be interpreted as indicating that they have disappointed adults and that they are of little worth.

On the other hand, because girls tend to be better at 'playing school' or 'looking busy' and are more likely to want to please the teacher, they run the risk of being rewarded for learning to underachieve and for being inconspicuous.

This is why feedback needs to encourage girls and build them up. But girls also need to be challenged when they are underperforming and be given reassurances that the problems can be remedied.

Give boys and girls something to EAT

Telling children that they are clever and praising them simply for their achievement might buoy them up in the short term but it can instil beliefs that make them vulnerable. Both boys and girls need to get the message that success is not simply about in-born talent or ability. Our feedback must put the emphasis on how they have or have not improved rather than how clever they are.

Give both boys and girls something to **EAT** by focusing on three things:

Effort (How hard you think the pupil has worked – or not.)

Achievement (How pleased you are at the progress they have made –
'I knew you could do this!' or disappointment at lack of progress –
'I know you can do better'.)

Technique (The strategies that pupils have used to be successful and/or the
strategies they need to use to do even better.)

Balance two kinds of feedback

To be motivated and effective learners we all need two kinds of feedback:

- **Descriptive feedback** that is honest and accurate, that lets us know how well we are doing and what we need to do to improve
- **Supportive feedback** that builds our confidence and helps us to believe that we can improve

Evidence suggests that a majority of males (around 60%) have a preference for giving and receiving descriptive feedback and a majority of females (around 60%) have a preference for giving and receiving supportive feedback.

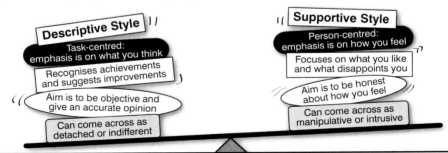

Descriptive Style

- Task-centred: emphasis is on what you think
- Recognises achievements and suggests improvements
- Aim is to be objective and give an accurate opinion
- Can come across as detached or indifferent

Supportive Style

- Person-centred: emphasis is on how you feel
- Focuses on what you like and what disappoints you
- Aim is to be honest about how you feel
- Can come across as manipulative or intrusive

Supportive but not too kind

It's important to ensure that our supportive feedback is not too kind. Teachers who have a supportive style may not challenge enough. They may try to insulate boys and, perhaps to a greater extent, girls from failure by:

- Setting easy work
- Offering unsolicited help
- Giving praise for easy success
- Showing pity following failure

All of these are counterproductive as pupils need to be able to deal with failure. If they realise that a teacher is protecting them from failure they will assume the teacher doesn't believe they have the ability to succeed.

Descriptive but not too judgemental

It's important to ensure that our descriptive feedback is not too judgemental. Teachers who have a descriptive style may not be supportive enough and may try to challenge girls and, perhaps to a greater extent, boys to succeed by:

- Putting too much emphasis on performance
- Giving too many early judgements
- Making public comparisons
- Giving no feedback at all when work is poor

All these are counterproductive, particularly when pupils are into comparing themselves with each other. The focus needs to be on how to improve, not simply on how well you have done.

Less praise, more encouragement

As teachers, we need to recognise some of the problems with **praise**.

- Both genders want feedback, but they want it to be good and they don't know if it's going to be good until they get it

- Many teenage boys pretend they don't want public praise from a teacher, while teenage girls may find it hard to accept, and worry that they have to live up to it

- Some teachers are tempted to give empty 'plastic' praise to seek compliance. Others give conditional praise to seek conformity

We can overcome some of these problems by focusing instead on **encouragement**.

- Praise often comes at the end; encouragement can be given at any time

- Students often have to earn praise; encouragement can be a gift, given for nothing, or for making an effort

- Praise often teaches students to please the teacher; encouragement values you for being yourself

- Praise is often vague; encouragement can be more explicit and informative

Don't be fooled by loud boys

Boys have a strong need to be capable and they want to show off their ability, but their tendency to compare themselves against others may lead them to opt out when they feel that they are not capable of succeeding. They tend to protect themselves from failure by making out they don't care and trying to look smart. This can be why boys don't ask for help or why criticism appears to go in one ear and out the other.

However, don't be fooled by loud boys who appear not to want feedback. It's easy to mistake their lack of confidence for apathy or arrogance and respond in the wrong way. Remember, boys may have a strong need to be capable and stand out but they also have a strong need to fit in and get along.

Don't be fooled by quiet girls

Girls' confidence in their own ability can be just as vulnerable as boys', but they tend to react differently. Rather than acting up or acting out they tend to protect their ability by keeping their heads down and trying to do their best. Unlike the boys, they don't play up or demand the teacher's attention but they do feel under great pressure to succeed.

Don't be fooled by quiet girls who appear not to want feedback. It's particularly important that these girls are given feedback which helps them to realise that their ability is changeable and that if they use the right strategies they will not only succeed but become more able.

It can be difficult sometimes to accept that these girls need this kind of feedback and to understand that as well as fitting in they also want to stand out and be their own person. They need feedback that helps them develop a greater sense of individuality without turning them into egocentric males.

Fewer judgements, more opinions

As teachers we have to make judgements. But a good way to deal with the issues around praise and criticism is to give **fewer judgements** and **more opinions**. Judgements often get in the way of relationships, particularly when you receive them from someone in authority. Indeed, there is some research to show that what irritates teenage boys and girls about their parents more than anything else is being judged.

When you express an opinion, use 'I' statements which describe your experience of the person rather than 'you' statements which describe the other person's attributes. 'I' statements come across as more real, more sincere and more original. They are also not attributive and although people can disagree with them they cannot say they are not true.

Instead of:	Use:
'Your behaviour is unacceptable.'	*'I am disappointed with your behaviour, I know you can do much better.'*
'Your work is really good.'	*'I am really pleased at how well you have tackled this task.'*

Sharing what you personally are thinking and feeling with boys and girls is a good way of connecting with them and building relationships.

Show appreciation and admiration

When you **appreciate** someone you let them know that they have given you something that you value. It is something that you, as a teacher, are happy to have or feel you have benefited from having; namely their behaviour, their effort, their progress, their success.

When you **admire** someone you are able to enter their world and find yourself instructed and inspired by them. Instead of conveying the message *'you are good'* it conveys the message *'I value you; I value what you are doing'*. It demonstrates positive regard and it involves taking a risk, sharing something of yourself.

> *'I am really pleased at how well you have done.'*
> *'I enjoyed reading your essay and I like the way you have laid it out.'*
> *'I admire the progress you have made.'*

There will, of course, be times when you need to show disappointment:
'I am disappointed with your report. You have not put as much work into it as usual. I know you can do better.'

Be specific and direct

Use specific language to describe what you appreciate, admire or are disappointed about. Don't talk about your *feeling* about what a person did; instead describe what the person *actually did* to cause you to feel that way.

Also, communicate your appreciation, admiration or your disappointment directly to the person, not to others about the person.

Make sure you own your feelings, so instead of saying: *'You make me feel...'* say: *'When you do... I feel...'*

> Your feelings need to be **communicated directly** to the person, not to others about the person, and your language needs to be **specific**.

Appreciate and admire both genders

Boys want to be appreciated and admired for standing out. Admire their wit, their confidence, their energy, their courage, their risk-taking and their ability at sport.

Girls want to be appreciated and admired for fitting in. Admire that they are thoughtful, empathetic, conscientious, sensitive and their ability to listen.

However, you can go to town on appreciation and admiration that crosses the gender stereotypes. So make sure that you also:

- Appreciate and admire **girls** for their wit, their confidence, their energy, their courage, their risk-taking and their ability at sport
- Appreciate and admire **boys** for being thoughtful, empathetic, conscientious and sensitive and for their ability to listen

Note: when giving both boys and girls feedback about their courage, convey to them that courage is not *resistance* to fear or the *absence* of fear but the ***mastery*** of fear.

Competition, rewards and grades

Most young boys enjoy risk-taking and find competition highly motivating, as long as they think they can win or at least not lose face; it can be a double-edged sword if they think it will expose them.

Young girls may need some encouragement to take the right kinds of risks, and may need to develop greater comfort with open competition than we realise, given that we live in a highly competitive world. Girls tend to bring competition and collaboration together more subtly than boys and may even need to practise competing in single gender groups (see next section).

Try the following strategies to help both genders deal with and enjoy competition:

- Have pupils compete with their own past performances
- Have pupils record their own improvements and progress
- Arrange occasional group/class competitions so pupils experience winning and losing as part of a group
- Ensure that all pupils experience winning and losing
- Encourage open discussions about what it feels like to win and lose

Ensure you emphasise improvement

Whatever feedback you give to boys or girls and however you give that feedback, put the emphasis on improvement rather than on the achievement of absolute standards of performance.

Instead of giving pupils a grade on every piece of work give them a plus or a minus or an equals depending on how it compares to the last piece of work they did. This can work for all students, but bright pupils who want to cruise hate it!

Where the feedback you give has to include a grade, score, level or mark, encourage both boys and girls to focus on how well they have done against their own previous score and how they can do better next time.

Avoid the public announcement of individual grades. It can encourage pupils to focus on being top of the class or getting better marks than their friends. And if they don't think this is possible, they may give up rather than try to improve on their own previous performance.

Gender,
Motivation
and Learning

 Connecting
with Boys
and Girls

 Being in
Control for
Boys and Girls

 Involving Boys
and Girls in
their Learning

 Giving Boys and
Girls Effective
Feedback

 Separate or
Together?

Separate
or Together

Single gender schooling

Co-education is by far the most common model of schooling across the world, which is why this Pocketbook has focused on how to work with boys and girls in mixed gender classes.

But there are those who feel strongly about the merits of single gender schools or single gender classes, especially in the adolescent years. Their argument is that single gender schools and classes lead to:

- Better examination results
- Improved attendance
- Fewer discipline referrals
- A better attitude to school

This section looks briefly at the arguments for and against co-education and at when and how to use gender as a means of making up groups in co-educational schools and classrooms.

The arguments for and against

The arguments for and against single gender schools or single gender classes within co-educational schools are outlined below.

	For	Against
For Boys	Adolescent boys focus more: they stop posturing to compete for and impress girls	Girls can have a civilising influence on boys
	Boys can be more expressive and more willing to share their feelings	Girls can help and encourage boys to collaborate
For Girls	Adolescent girls don't feel the need to dumb down to feed male egos	Girls learn to deal with macho male egos
	Girls can be more assertive	Boys can help and encourage girls to take risks and compete
For Both	You can treat both boys and girls more appropriately	Single gender classes reinforce gender stereotypes
	Both boys and girls can relax and drop the gender roles	Boys and girls have to work with the other gender in adult life; why separate them in adolescence?

What the research says

A great deal of research has been carried out into the merits and demerits of single gender schooling across the world. The results are uncertain, but they come to the following broad conclusions:

- There is no indication that single gender schooling harms students academically
- Low-achieving students probably gain most and high-achieving students least
- Any suggestions that there are negative effects on boys' and girls' social development are speculative
- There is some evidence that single gender schools develop in students more positive attitudes toward certain traditionally male or female subjects
- Findings that girls benefit more than boys from single sex schooling have been undercut by studies that show the opposite

The rest of this section is designed to help teachers decide what choices to make in co-educational schools where there is flexibility to choose whether to separate boys and girls or teach them together.

Mixed gender pairs

Many teachers have experimented with mixed gender pairs and groups, especially in secondary schools. Research suggests that it can reduce disruption but there are also potential dangers with this approach as outlined below.

What girls think
- Generally not positive
- Feel uncomfortable
- Feel they are held back
- Think boys just copy their work

What boys think
- Generally more positive
- Fewer distractions from friends
- Tempted to chat girls up
- Do admit it gives them a chance to copy

However, as the example on page 117 shows, where a teacher is committed and skilful in their use of mixed gender pairs, it's an approach that can pay dividends.

Collaboration doesn't just happen

One thing is clear. Effective collaboration across the genders, especially in the adolescent years, will not happen unless the teacher believes it is important and is both assertive and skilful in bringing it about.

Teachers who are good at fostering collaborative learning in general, as well as specifically across the genders, tend to have the following characteristics in common.

They:
- Have high expectations of what pupils can learn together in pairs and groups
- Don't underestimate the difficulties of boys and girls working together
- Are prepared to open up discussions even in challenging classrooms
- Role model more equal dialogue in whole-class lessons
- Build community by devising short, focused talk-based tasks for pairs
- Emphasise 'learning partners' and use ground rules for paired working
- Give careful thought to choosing the learning partners

Mixed gender pairs in Maths

A Maths teacher was renowned in her school for using mixed gender pairs in all her classes (ages 12-18). She seated pupils in boy/girl pairs, alphabetically. When she had a class for the first time she explained why she was doing this. She pointed out that she wanted her students to be able to work with a whole range of people to prepare them for life after school.

Throughout the year she monitored how each pair was working together. If she felt a certain pair was not working she reshuffled the whole class. She normally did this by rows – boys or girls in the first row move to the second, the second row moves to the third and so on. She tended to change the seating every two or three months.

She found that with some classes, the boy/girl arrangement could also tap into the natural competitive element between boys and girls at secondary school age. Also, by not allowing peer groups of the same sex to sit together, the tendency to withdraw from classroom participation in the presence of friends was removed.

When to separate boys & girls

There are times when it is sensible to give adolescent and pre-adolescent boys and girls information and talk time without the other gender present. This may apply not only to sexual issues but to a range of social and personal issues which can affect boys and girls in our society in very different ways.

In our culture there are different pressures on boys and girls and they respond in different ways. Also girls bully and respond to bullying in different ways.

In our culture there is pressure on girls to:
- Dress provocatively
- Focus on body image
- Look good
- Be thin

In our culture there is pressure on boys to:
- Be respected
- Be tough
- Be cool
- Avoid looking weak

Girls often respond by:
- Looking first at their own inadequacies
- Harming themselves
- Trying to wreck other people's relationships
- Ignoring
- Teasing or backstabbing

Boys often respond by:
- Fighting and/or fleeing
- Keeping their problems to themselves – or blowing up
- Damaging others and then buttoning up

Just girls

You can use single gender groups to encourage girls to take the lead, to argue and compete. Girls enjoy doing these things but they are areas in which girls may need more help and practice than we realise.

It can be a good idea to ask girls what is important to them without boys around.

Single gender groups can provide an opportunity to draw their attention to women's rights and women's issues, to interest them in social injustice and to help them consider how they can bring about change and influence others in positive ways.

Single gender groups can be an effective way of helping girls to consider and develop leadership abilities and attitudes. They can look at examples of female role models and how they have shaped change in positive ways.

Just boys

You can use single gender groups to encourage boys to talk about their feelings. Showing your feelings, especially when things go wrong, can be seen by boys as a sign of weakness, particularly when there are girls around. Single gender groups can provide boys with a safe environment where they can share their feelings when things go wrong.

One way to do this is to help them develop an emotional vocabulary by using word lists like the one opposite but often it's a good idea not to be too direct with boys. Instead of asking a boy *'How did that make you feel?'* ask him about what he did or what he plans to do about the problem.

Develop an emotional vocabulary

Happy	Sad	Angry	Valued	Surprised	Afraid	Hurt	Inadequate
calm	alone	annoyed	accepted	amazed	cornered	aggrieved	ashamed
carefree	ashamed	bitter	admired	astonished	desperate	cheated	awkward
cheerful	bored	disgusted	capable	dismayed	fearful	defeated	defective
delighted	dismal	frustrated	competent	flabbergasted	frightened	devastated	helpless
encouraged	disappointed	furious	confident	mystified	hurt	disappointed	ignorant
excited	gloomy	grumpy	loved	puzzled	intimidated	heartbroken	inferior
glad	glum	mad	proud	rattled	nervous	ignored	incapable
overjoyed	miserable	resentful	respected	shaken	scared	put down	incompetent
lucky	sullen	riled	special	shocked	timid	upset	rejected
thrilled	wretched	upset	trusted	thunderstruck	worried	wounded	useless

Discuss gender from very early on

Children become aware of gender differences around the age of two.

From very early on, whether you are teaching in single or mixed gender classes, find opportunities to talk about typical differences between boys and girls and challenge the stereotypes. For example, expose boys and girls to people from all walks of life who do not fit traditional stereotypes: female joiners, male nurses, male receptionists, women architects.

When you can, talk about gender issues in mixed groups. One way to do this is to get pupils to carry out gender surveys. The first example on the following page is suitable for younger pupils and the second for adolescents.

Discuss gender issues in mixed groups

1. Favourite words (primary)

Ask pupils the following two questions:

> 'What are your five favourite words?'

> 'Why do you like each word?'

Then ask them to swap notes in mixed gender pairs and report back on the similarities and differences.

2. What do you look for in a friend? (secondary)

Each pupil asks 10 males and 10 females what they look for in a friend and records their responses. They are then listed in the following categories:

- What boys say to boys

- What girls say to girls

- What boys say to girls

- What girls say to boys

The class generates a top ten list for all four categories and discusses any patterns that emerge.

Consider important questions together

Once adolescents feel comfortable with cross-gender discussion, encourage them to consider questions that might be of greater immediate interest and concern to the opposite gender.

Questions to pose girls that might be of more immediate interest to boys	Questions to pose boys that might be of more immediate interest to girls
When has been your greatest moment of success?	What do you like most in other people?
What do you want to do that you have not yet done?	What do you dislike most in other people?
Are there any changes you would like to make in your life?	Would you mind being different from other people?
Which of your possessions do you value most?	In what ways are you like other people of your age?
	In what ways are you different from other people?

A school policy on gender

The key message from this Pocketbook is that we should not downplay the importance of gender differences. Nor should we focus exclusively on 'the problem with boys' or 'the problem with girls' or seek to eradicate gender differences by getting boys to act like girls or vice-versa. Rather:

We should teach boys that there are many ways to be a man and teach girls that there are many ways to be a woman.

Any school policy on gender needs to recognise that the factors influencing gender are complex and should encourage teachers to examine the following kinds of questions:

- What ideas about men and women do young people bring to school and how do these ideas manifest themselves in the classroom and the playground?
- What kinds of role models does the school want and expect from its teachers?
- What kinds of activities should pupils be involved in to help them discuss gender issues and question gender stereotypes?

I hope the *Boys, Girls & Learning Pocketbook* will help schools and teachers to formulate such a policy and help teachers to make it work in the classroom.

Recommended reading

Bringing the Best Out in Boys:
Communication Strategies for Teachers
by Lucinda Neall. Paul Chapman Educational
Publishing, 2003

The Essential Difference: Men, Women and
the Extreme Male Brain
by Simon Baron-Cohen. Allen Lane, 2003

I only Say This Because I Love You
by Deborah Tannen. Virago Press, 2002

Mindset: the New Psychology of Success
by Carol Dweck. Random House, 2006

Motivating Every Learner
by Alan McLean. Sage, 2009

People Skills
by Robert Bolton. Simon and Schuster, 1979

Self-Theories: Their Role in Motivation,
Personality and Development (Essays in
Social Psychology)
by Carol Dweck. Psychology Press, 2000

And the following Teachers' Pocketbooks:

Assessment & Learning
by Ian Smith, 2007

Drama for Learning
by Brian Radcliffe, 2007

Effective Classroom Communication
by Richard Churches, 2010

Growth Mindset
by Barry Hymer & Mike Gershon, 2014

Independent Learning
by Peter Anstee, 2015